Coloured by You

Dedication

For Brin & Lily who keep us young and constantly dreaming.

Special thanks

To Wendy for reconnecting with her passion to draw again.
To our friends and family who support us on our creative adventures.

For more DOODLELovely, visit **www.doodlelovely.com**

DOODLED IN

CANADA

>>>> Coloured by You <<<<

OH CANADA

Canada is a colourful nation. Our people, our history, our landscape.
It's a country where your imagination can flourish, your creativity can soar.

This book celebrates Canada's 150th birthday by taking you on
a tour through some of the places, people, and things that have shaped
our identity, our pride, and our dreams.

Doodled in Canada puts you in the role of artist, interpreting Canada's symbols
with your own rainbow of colour, guided by your true north spirit.

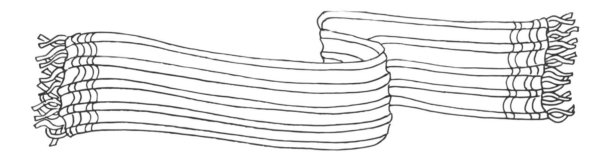

If you lined up all the scarves owned
by Canadians, they would encircle the globe
in one soft snuggly hug.

The coldest day ever recorded in Canada happened in Snag, Yukon on February 3, 1947.
The temperature dropped to a very chilly -63°C, even without a wind chill!

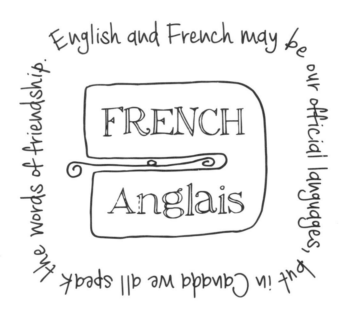

English and French may be our official languages, but in Canada we all speak the words of friendship.

FRENCH
Anglais

French and English officially became the two languages of Canada on September 11, 1972. New Brunswick is the only officially bilingual province.

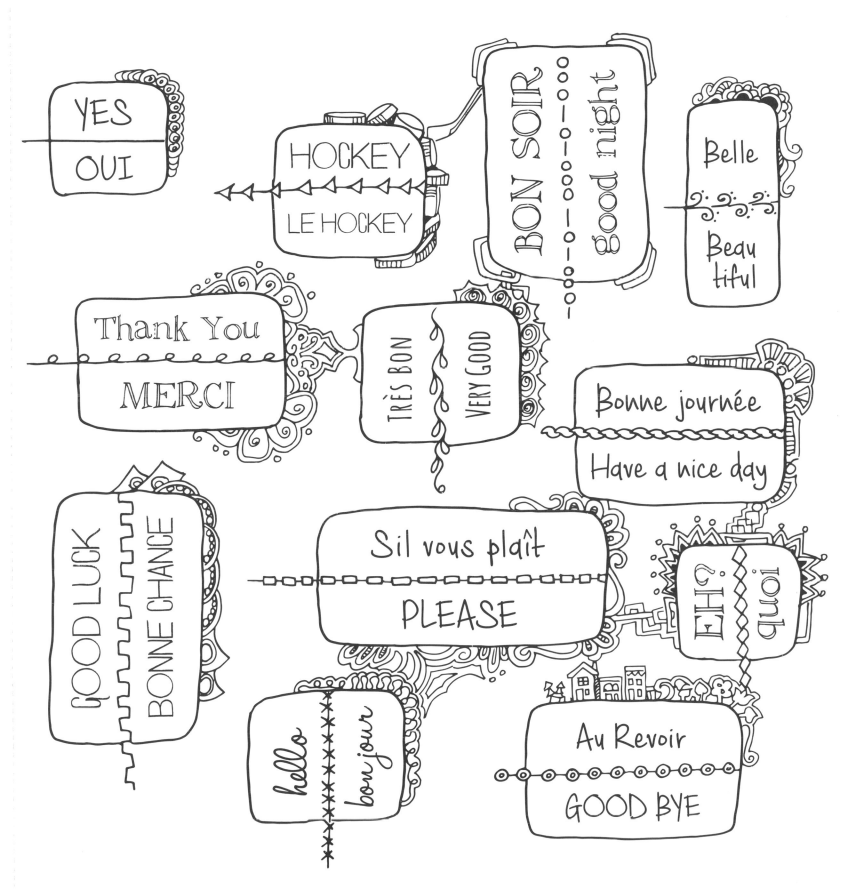

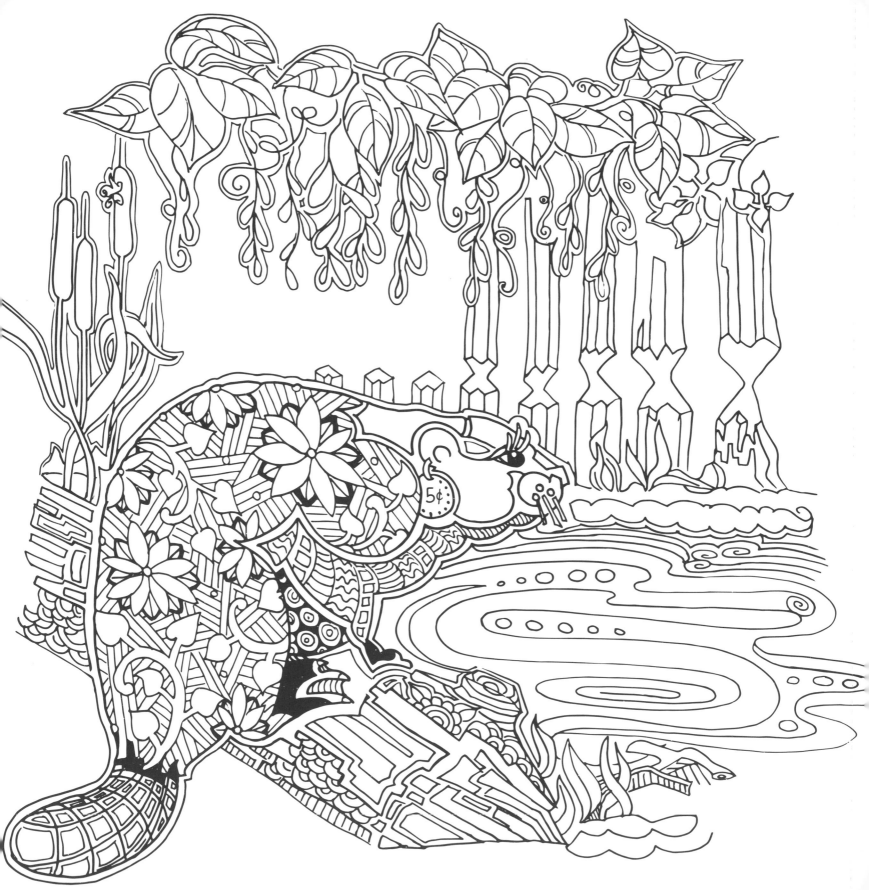

If the beaver is as busy as they say, aren't they worth more than 5 cents?

The beaver is the largest rodent in North America and while they may seem to
waddle on land, they are strong and fast swimmers that can see underwater.
The beaver is a hardworking engineer, building dams and lodges out of trees and mud.
Each beaver cuts down about 216 trees a year!

To the outside world, winter defines us. But in truth, it is winter that refines us.

Snowflakes are ice crystals that form in the clouds when water vapour freezes. Every snowflake has six sides and there are 35 different shapes of snowflakes!

There is a paddle for every pace.
And it's always peaceful.

The flow of the river and the glide
of the canoe brings you one stroke closer to the
natural world... and your Canadian soul.

*The canoe was essential to Canada's Indigenous Peoples for hunting,
transportation, and survival. On the Pacific Coast they were dug out from the massive
cedar trees, while birch bark was often used in the rest of Canada.*

One part goofy-looking, the moose is
all parts majestic; a thriving survivor and gentle
giant of the Canadian wilderness.

One of the largest animals in North America, the moose likes to live near lakes and
marshy areas of the boreal forest. They grow new antlers every year that can span between
120-150cm wide. Moose use their antlers to fight during mating season.

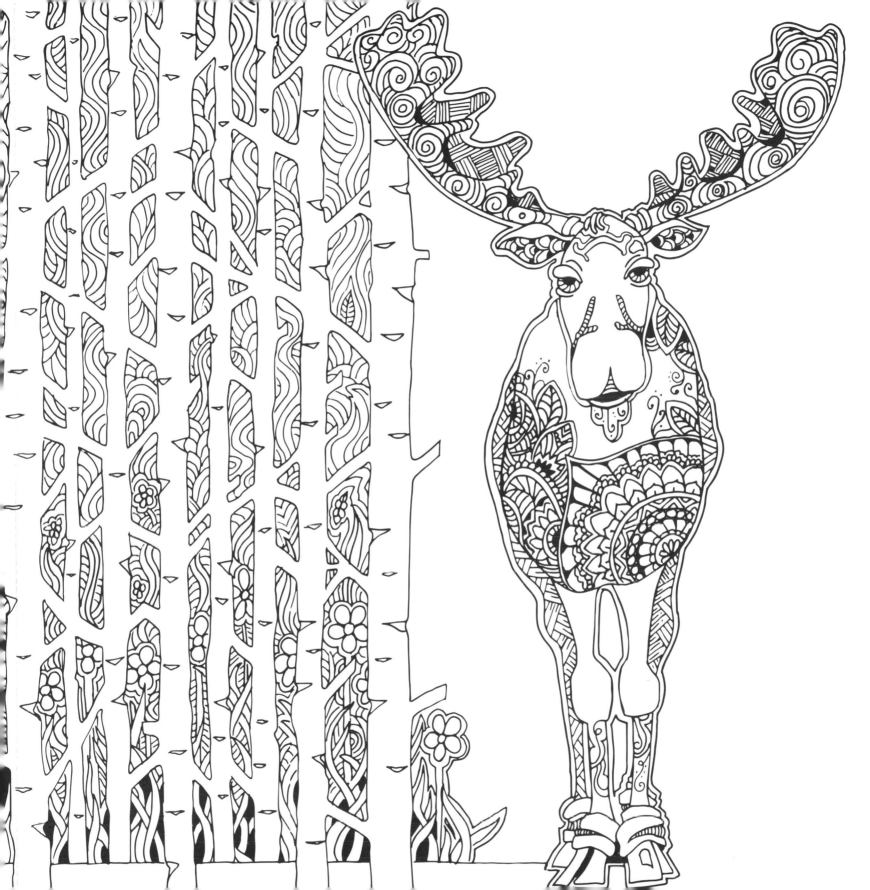

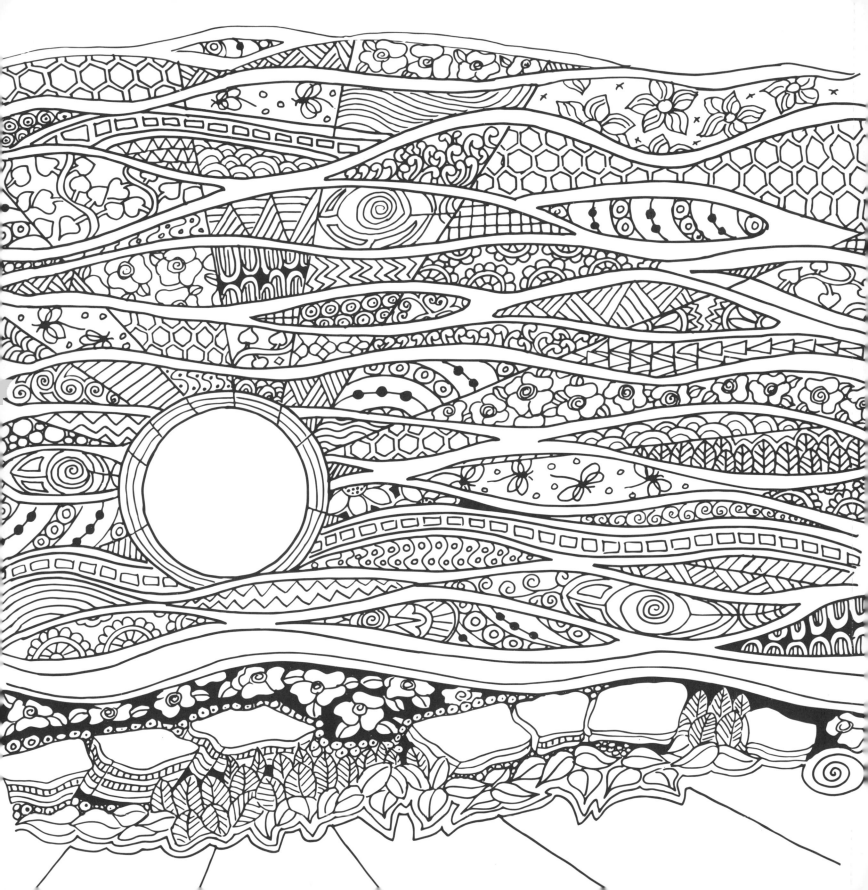

Beyond just a land of ice and snow, Canada's north is a magical place where the summer sun shines at midnight and where the winter skies are alive with dancing colour of the northern lights.

During the summer months in Canada's north, you can still see the sun even at midnight. Which means you can play, go for a hike, or read a book outside late into the evening without needing a flashlight!

Canada's motto is A Mari usque ad Mare

"From Sea to Sea"

Canada's Coat of Arms was assigned by royal proclamation of King George V in 1921.
It reflects symbols of both France and England with lions, a harp, fleurs-de-lis, a unicorn,
and, of course, maple leaves for Canada.

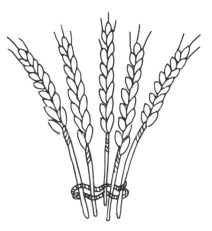

Time may have moved on, but the grain elevators
of the Prairies still stand proudly along the rail lines;
a vanishing icon of agriculture in North America.

*In the early 20th century, almost every prairie town along a railway had at least one
or two grain elevators and by the 1930's there were more than 5,000 across
the Canadian Prairies. They were essential for storing grain from farms until it could
be transported by train to markets across the country.*

There is no greater thrill than to slip, slide, and scream with glee down a snowy hill. ooooo

Originally built by Canada's Indigenous Peoples to transport people and supplies, toboggans are made of long wooden slats that are bent into a 'J' shape. It's different from a sleigh or sled because it doesn't have runners or skis on the bottom — it slides directly on the snow.

We play it, watch it, talk it, teach it, scream it, win it.

The game of hockey is said to have originated in about 1800. It was played by students of King's College School on a frozen pond in Windsor, Nova Scotia.

It may proudly house the spirit of Canadian democracy, but Parliament Hill is also home to 53 majestic bells, a stray cat sanctuary, and fantastical, mischievous gargoyles.

When Canada officially became a nation in 1867, Queen Victoria chose Ottawa as the new capital city. Representatives from across the country moved into the grand Parliament Buildings to begin the business of building a nation.

Large v-shaped migratory flocks of majestic Canada geese are often a

sign of a season passing as they leave for the fall and return again in spring.

The Canada Goose has about 13 different calls, and baby geese, called goslings, start communicating with their parents while they're still in the egg!

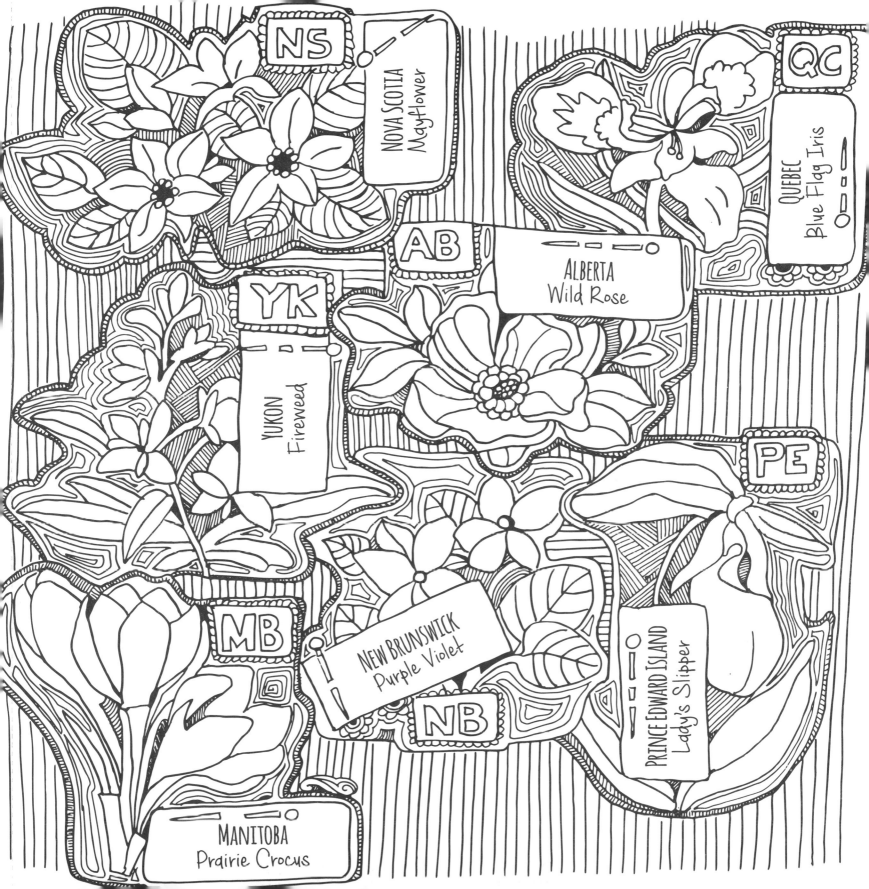

Sharp red serge, smart Stetson hat, and shiny boots astride a handsome black horse, the legend of the Mounties is that they "always get their man."

The Royal Canadian Mounted Police, also known as "Mounties" have been a global symbol of Canadian law and order since 1873.

The maple leaf is our national symbol of unity, tolerance, and peace. It also symbolizes the liquid joy of sweet maple syrup and happy bellies.

The maple leaf became a symbol of Canada in the early 1700's.
It is featured on our flag and Canadians travelling around the world are instantly recognized and welcomed at the sight of the red leaf.

Warm and woolly, mitts and toques are the
secret to enjoying a Canadian winter.

*What makes mittens so toasty warm is because your fingers stay together inside the mitten,
generating body heat as opposed to gloves which separate each finger on its own. Brrr!*

Carved from a tall red cedar and traditionally painted red, black, and blue, the totem pole is a proud monument of the lives and beliefs of the Indigenous Peoples of Canada's Northwest coast.

The Inuit of Canada's North use rocks to create Inukshuks. They are used for navigation, as a sign of food left for travellers, or to mark places of spiritual significance.

Behind the pretty fishing villages that line the shores of Eastern Canada are stories of the adventure, travel, danger, and triumph of life lived on the sea.

The biggest lobster ever caught came from Nova Scotia in 1977 — it weighed more than 44 lbs and was thought to be about 100 years old.

For more than 200 years, the Hudson's Bay blanket
with its cheerful stripes of green, red, yellow, and indigo
is still popular, influencing fashion and design.

*The Hudson's Bay point blanket is to this day a warm symbol of Canada's
evolution as a nation. First introduced into the fur trade in 1780 as a valuable
commodity for trade with Canada's Indigenous Peoples.*

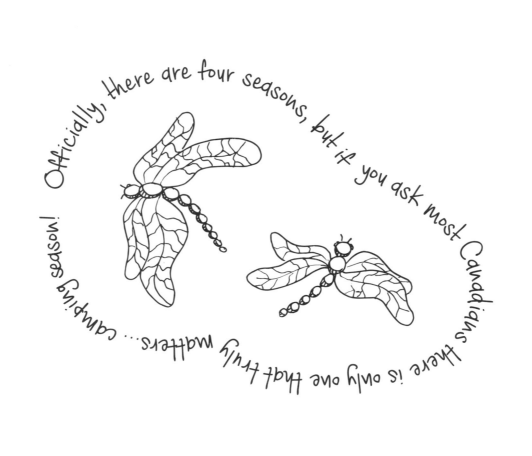

Officially, there are four seasons, but if you ask most Canadians there is only one that truly matters... camping season!

There are four seasons in Canada: spring, summer, fall, winter. The time when each season starts and ends varies greatly, depending on where you live in this very large country.

From coast to coast to coast, Canada's cities are as diverse as its people. The architecture reflects a pride of place, an optimistic energy, and a sense of legacy unique to each.

The top four cities in Canada are Toronto, Ontario; Montreal, Quebec; Vancouver, British Columbia, and Calgary, Alberta.

During the 2002 Salt Lake City Olympics,
Canadian ice maker, Trent Evans, secretly placed a loonie
in the ice to wish Team Canada hockey team luck
against Team USA in the gold medal game. Team Canada
won 5-2 so that really was one lucky loonie!

In 1987, the Royal Canadian Mint introduced a one dollar coin decorated with a loon
on one side and it quickly earned the nickname "loonie". When the two dollar coin followed in 1996,
the nickname "toonie" was a natural fit. Evidence of the famous Canadian sense of humour?

A beacon of hope, a cry of warning,
the lighthouses of Canada's shorelines are proud
guardians of sailors and seafarers.

*Built in 1758, the oldest surviving lighthouse in North America is on
Sambro Island, Nova Scotia, at the entrance to Halifax Harbour.*

Few things unite us more than the salty, cheesy goodness of poutine or the sweet happiness of a drizzle of maple syrup.

Maple syrup is made by tapping the sap of maple trees and boiling it down for many hours. It takes about 40 litres of maple sap to make 1 litre of maple syrup.

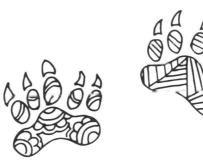

Traditionally a house made of snow to protect the Inuit from the Arctic's harsh conditions, the igloo has become the ultimate spot for Canadian winter fun.

More than just cuddly good looks, the polar bear is an excellent swimmer, even in the frigid Arctic waters, and has a sense of smell so strong it can detect a seal's breathing hole in the ice from up to a kilometre away!

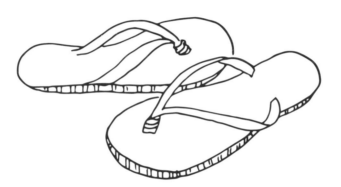

It's the magical chair of summer where the sun shines,
people exhale, nature abounds, and we are happy.

*The Muskoka chair can be seen on decks, docks, and shorelines across Canada
in a rainbow of colour, just waiting for that perfect summer day.*

HAPPY BIRTHDAY CANADA

Bon anniversaire

YOUR LIST OF ALL THINGS CANADIAN

When you think of Canada, what things come to your mind?

....

....

....

....

....

....

....

....

....

....

....

Use this space to create images of Canada,
from colourful coast to coast to coast.

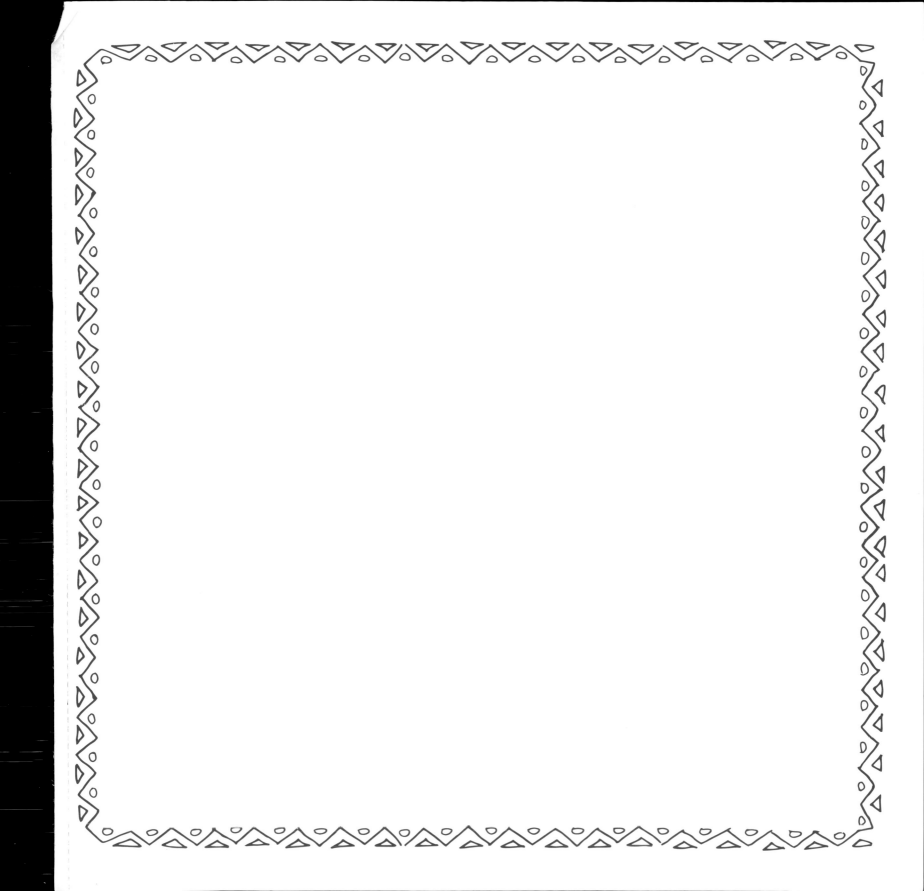

⨯⨯⨯⨯ THREE YOUNG Canadians ⨯⨯⨯⨯

WENDY BURNS MORRISON ~ Illustrator

Born an Ottawa girl, the gift of Canada offered endless possibilities. Drawing became her passion, graphic art her career, and recently Cape Breton Island, Nova Scotia her home. Wendy retired the mouse in favour of a pen after 35 years. Her dedication, spirit and humour spring from a long love of Canada. Her drawings... they are inspired by Brin and Lily who call her Grammy.

MELISSA LLOYD ~ Graphic Designer

A dynamic creator, whose heart is by the sea in her home in Hubbards, Nova Scotia. Melissa is inspired by all things Canadian. Her enhanced vision is shaped by a worldly background, and more than a touch of energy. Melissa always seeks to achieve things that really matter and strives for greater happiness for herself and those around her.

JENNIFER FAULKNER ~ Writer

Jennifer Faulkner is a writer living in Halifax, Nova Scotia. She once drove across Canada with her dog, Bras d'Or (named after the lakes in Cape Breton) from Whitehorse, Yukon to Marion Bridge, Nova Scotia. She's still waiting for someone to write a folk song about it.